T0016442

NAVY SEALS

BY SUSAN B. KATZ

Apex is distributed by North Star Editions:
sales@northstareditions.com | 888-417-0195

Produced for Apex by Red Line Editorial.

Photographs ©: Shutterstock Images, cover, 1, 10–11, 14–15, 16–17, 18, 22–23; iStockphoto, 4–5, 6–7, 8, 8–9, 13, 20–21, 29; Denis Poroy/AP Images, 24; United States Navy/Wikimedia Commons, 25; United States Navy/Wikimedia Commons, 26–27

Library of Congress Control Number: 2022901416

ISBN
978-1-63738-309-4 (hardcover)
978-1-63738-345-2 (paperback)
978-1-63738-413-8 (ebook pdf)
978-1-63738-381-0 (hosted ebook)

Printed in the United States of America
Mankato, MN
082022

NOTE TO PARENTS AND EDUCATORS

Apex books are designed to build literacy skills in striving readers. Exciting, high-interest content attracts and holds readers' attention. The text is carefully leveled to allow students to achieve success quickly. Additional features, such as bolded glossary words for difficult terms, help build comprehension.

TABLE OF CONTENTS

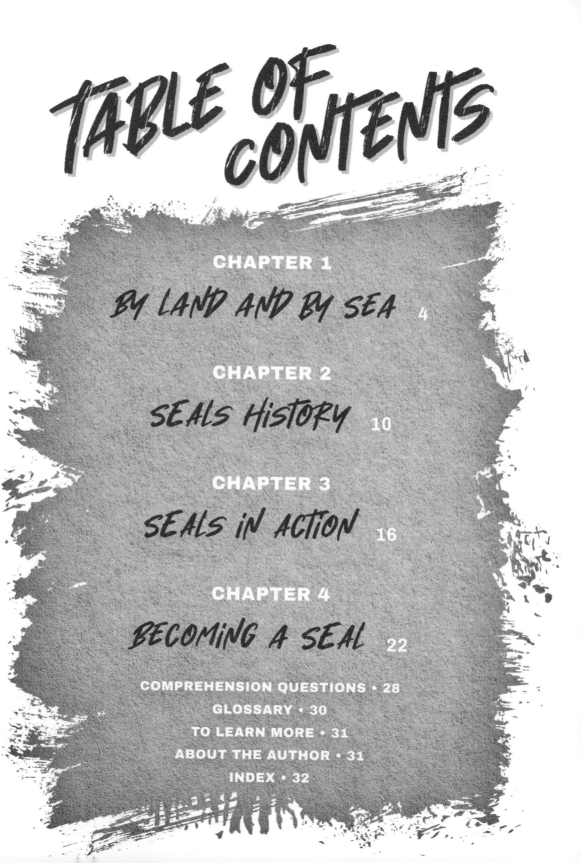

CHAPTER 1

BY LAND AND BY SEA 4

CHAPTER 2

SEALS HISTORY 10

CHAPTER 3

SEALS IN ACTION 16

CHAPTER 4

BECOMING A SEAL 22

COMPREHENSION QUESTIONS • 28
GLOSSARY • 30
TO LEARN MORE • 31
ABOUT THE AUTHOR • 31
INDEX • 32

BY LAND AND BY SEA

Navy SEALs crawl out of a **submarine**. They put on diving gear. Then they jump into the ocean. The water is cold. The SEALs swim quickly.

Navy SEALs may spend weeks or months inside a submarine for a mission.

Finally, the SEALs reach land. They crawl onto the beach. Then, they head toward an enemy city. To get there, the SEALs sneak across a desert. They climb a mountain, too.

SEALs can take out their targets from the water or from land.

SEALs must move
without being spotted.

At the city, the SEALs take out their target. Then the swift SEALs leave as quickly and quietly as they came.

Helicopters help SEALs get in and out of enemy land quickly without getting caught.

HELP FROM ABOVE

Navy SEALs work in teams. Some SEALs parachute down from helicopters. Other SEALs stay inside and keep watch. They look out for enemy fire.

CHAPTER 2

SEALS HISTORY

The Navy SEALs are a **special forces** group. They were founded in 1962. At first, they did only **maritime** missions. Later, they fought on land and in water.

Navy SEALs often use small, fast boats to travel on the water.

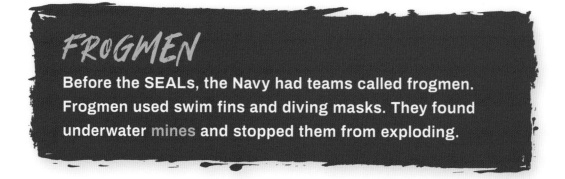

FROGMEN

Before the SEALs, the Navy had teams called frogmen. Frogmen used swim fins and diving masks. They found underwater mines and stopped them from exploding.

Navy SEALs went on to fight in several wars for the United States. Other **operations** included rescuing Americans in other countries.

SEALs wear gear to help them breathe and see underwater. ▶

During the early 2000s, SEALs teamed up with the US Army for missions in Iraq.

FAST FACT

At first, only men were allowed to become Navy SEALs. The first woman became a Navy SEAL in 2021.

Navy SEALs once tricked Iraq's military. The SEALs made them think Iraq would be attacked by sea. But forces attacked Iraq by land instead. The surprise mission was a success.

CHAPTER 3

SEALS iN ACTION

SEALs do many types of operations today. They may get people out of dangerous places. Or they may capture enemies.

Navy SEALs are called to do secret or difficult missions.

Navy SEALs also gather information. They go behind enemy lines. They learn what the other side is planning to do. This helps the US military stop attacks.

SEALs often use gear and clothing that help them hide from enemies.

TEAM EFFORT

Navy SEALs are known for being fierce fighters. But for each SEAL who fights, others help in the background. Some send messages. Others keep watch from hilltops or airplanes.

Each SEAL focuses on a different skill. Some train in climbing or diving. Others give medical care.

The SEALs have a parachute team called the Leap Frogs.

CHAPTER 4

BECOMING A SEAL

Every SEAL team has a **commander**. This person leads two to four **platoons**. Each platoon includes 16 SEALs.

Each Navy SEAL platoon is broken up into smaller groups of SEALs.

As part of their training, SEALs learn to work together.

Becoming a SEAL is very difficult. First, people must pass boot camp. Then, they go to SEAL school. This training lasts more than a year.

TOUGH TRAINING

SEALs train for tough conditions. They stay in ice-cold water for eight minutes. They carry heavy logs over their heads. They practice working with little sleep.

SEALs must be fast and strong. They go through very hard training.

In their training, SEALs practice many skills. They swim and dive. They also learn to fight at night. SEALs may need all these skills for their missions.

FAST FACT

SEAL training is so tough that only one in five people pass.

SEALs go through lengthy weapons training.

COMPREHENSION QUESTIONS

Write your answers on a separate piece of paper.

1. Write a paragraph that explains the type of work Navy SEALs do.

2. Do you think fighting on land or in water would be harder? Why?

3. What does SEAL stand for?

    A. Sea, Air, and Land

    B. Sea, Earth, and Lakes

    C. Soldiers Even After Loss

4. Why would Navy SEALs keep watch from hilltops or airplanes?

    A. Being high up helps them stay warm.

    B. Being high up helps them see danger or enemies.

    C. Being high up helps enemies see them.

5. What does **swift** mean in this book?

Then the swift SEALs leave as quickly and quietly as they came.

    A. slow-moving

    B. fast-moving

    C. too small to see

6. What does **tough** mean in this book?

SEALs train for tough conditions. They stay in ice-cold water for eight minutes.

    A. warm and soft

    B. fun and easy

    C. hard or painful

Answer key on page 32.

GLOSSARY

commander
The leader of a military group.

maritime
Done by sea or in boats, not on land.

mines
Devices that are placed under the ground or water and that explode if bumped.

operations
Plans and actions made by the military.

parachute
To jump from high up while wearing fabric to slow one's fall.

platoons
Groups of the military who live, work, and fight together.

special forces
Groups of the military who get extra training and do work such as spying or surprise attacks.

submarine
A ship that can stay deep underwater for a long time.

TO LEARN MORE

BOOKS

Abdo, Kenny. *Navy SEALs.* Minneapolis: Abdo Publishing, 2019.

Eason, Sarah. *Navy SEALs: The Capture of Bin Laden!* Minneapolis: Bearport Publishing, 2021.

Pagel-Hogan, Elizabeth. *US Special Operations Forces Equipment and Vehicles.* Minneapolis: Abdo Publishing, 2021.

ONLINE RESOURCES

Visit **www.apexeditions.com** to find links and resources related to this title.

ABOUT THE AUTHOR

Susan B. Katz is an award-winning, Spanish bilingual author/ illustrator of more than 25 books. She is also a National Board Certified Teacher. Her father, Ray, is a Vietnam-era Air Force veteran.

INDEX

E

enemy, 6, 9, 16, 19

F

fight, 10, 12, 20, 26
founded, 10
frogmen, 12

I

Iraq, 15

L

land, 6–7, 10, 15

M

missions, 10, 26

O

operations, 12, 16

P

pirates, 19

S

skill, 20, 26
special forces, 10
submarine, 4

T

teams, 9, 12, 22
training, 24–26

W

wars, 12
water, 4, 7, 10, 25

ANSWER KEY:
1. Answers will vary; 2. Answers will vary; 3. A; 4. B; 5. B; 6. C